Original title:
Snow-Kissed Horizon

Copyright © 2024 Swan Charm
All rights reserved.

Author: Kene Elistrand
ISBN HARDBACK: 978-9916-79-804-1
ISBN PAPERBACK: 978-9916-79-805-8
ISBN EBOOK: 978-9916-79-806-5

Radiant Reflections in the Chill

In the quiet dawn, light breaks,
Whispers in frost, each breath shakes.
Trees shimmer with a silver lace,
Nature's mirror, a tranquil space.

A brook babbles, beneath icy blue,
Glimmers of gold in the morning dew.
Each ripple sings to the rising sun,
A dance of shadows, the day's begun.

Colors flicker on the canvas wide,
Sunlight spills where the shadows hide.
Footsteps crunch on the wintry ground,
In the heart of silence, peace is found.

Clouds drift lazily, soft and white,
Kissing the earth with a gentle light.
Birds take flight, on the frosty air,
Echoes of joy, a world so rare.

As day unfolds, warmth takes its claim,
Radiant reflections, never the same.
In the chill, there's a fiery glow,
A reminder of beauty, forever to grow.

Beneath the Arctic Lullaby

The world is hush, a blanket white,
Soft whispers drift in the frosty night.
Stars peek through the shimmering frost,
In silence, we ponder what's gained and lost.

Beneath the moon's tender, glowing ray,
Winter's charm sweeps the troubles away.
Each breath a cloud in the icy air,
A dance of dreams floating, free from care.

The northern lights paint tales untold,
A symphony of colors, bright and bold.
Nature's canvas, a sight to behold,
Wrapped in wonder, we feel consoled.

Frostbitten Tales of Serene Nights

In the quiet realm of the frosted glen,
Where stories linger, time's soft pen.
Whispers of frost weave tales of old,
Of moons and stars, of hearts and gold.

Each icy breath tells of ancient lore,
With every step on the crisp, cold floor.
Night covers all with a silver shawl,
A tranquil peace that beckons us all.

The trees stand tall, their branches bare,
Guardians of secrets in the chilling air.
Frostbitten tales, they softly share,
As dreams take flight, beyond compare.

Echoes of a Winter's Embrace

In winter's grasp, the world feels still,
Echoes of silence, a tranquil thrill.
Time drifts softly on frozen streams,
As twilight dances, igniting dreams.

The crunch of snow beneath my feet,
A crisp reminder, the moment sweet.
In every flake, a whispering grace,
The heart finds warmth in winter's embrace.

Stars flicker down from the velvet dusk,
The air, a blend of fresh and musk.
With every breath, we weave the dance,
In echoes of night, we find our chance.

Threads of Silver in the Sky

The heavens weep with threads of silver,
A tapestry that makes the heart quiver.
Each glistening star a distant spark,
Guiding lost souls through the dark.

Beneath the vast, enchanted expanse,
We lose ourselves in a timeless trance.
Moonlight drapes the earth in dreams,
Illuminating paths, or so it seems.

The night unfolds with a gentle sigh,
In the embrace of stars, we learn to fly.
With every glimmer, a wish takes flight,
Threads of silver weaving through the night.

Starlit Pathway Through Frozen Woods

Through frozen trees the starlight gleams,
A pathway glimmers with silver beams.
Whispers of night wrap the world in peace,
Nature's beauty gives the heart a tease.

Snowflakes dance in the cool, crisp air,
Each step taken, a wonder to share.
In silence deep, the shadows play,
With starlight guiding the lonely way.

Night's embrace brings a calming bliss,
In the woods where secrets softly kiss.
The moon above casts a gentle glow,
Leading us further where few dare to go.

Softly the frost lays a blanket white,
Transforming the world into pure delight.
An enchanting stroll through the night's serene,
With nature's wonders forever seen.

Frosted Wishes on the Wind

Wishes soar on the breeze so cold,
Tales of warmth on winter's fold.
Frosted petals dance in the air,
Silent prayers for those who care.

Each breath taken, a cloud appears,
Carried away, our hopes and fears.
Nature's canvas painted white,
A tapestry woven in winter's light.

Stars twinkle above with a gentle wink,
While rivers of ice softly sink.
Time stands still in the chill of night,
A moment captured, pure and bright.

Listen closely as wishes arrive,
On frosted winds they twist and thrive.
Each promise made in the quietest hush,
An echo of joy in the evening's rush.

Between Shadows and Glittering Light

Shadows linger where the light meets,
In whispers soft, the silence greets.
A dance of twilight under the stars,
Echoes of magic, healing scars.

Glimmers shine through branches bare,
Mysteries hidden, fresh winter air.
The world lies still in twilight's grasp,
As dreams emerge for our hands to clasp.

Footsteps crunch on the frosty ground,
A melody of nature's sound.
Between the dark and the shining bright,
We wander onward into the night.

Every star a wish, every shadow a fear,
In this embrace, the path is clear.
With hearts open wide, we take the chance,
Within this moment, we find our dance.

The Whispering Harmony of Winter's Frost

Winter's breath paints a world so pure,
In frosted hues, we feel the allure.
A whispering breeze tells tales untold,
Of moments cherished and memories bold.

Silver branches sway with grace,
Nature's rhythm sets the pace.
In the quiet, a song begins,
The harmony of frost lingers within.

Each flake falls softly, a brief embrace,
Gathering warmth in the coldest place.
With every sigh, the world transforms,
In winter's cradle, the heart warms.

Listen closely to the frozen air,
There's a melody hidden everywhere.
A soothing balm for weary souls,
In winter's arms, we feel it whole.

Whispers of Winter's Breath

Amidst the snow, the silence keeps,
A soft embrace, where shadows creep.
Crystals dance in gentle sighs,
Nature's hush beneath gray skies.

Beneath the trees, a blanket white,
Dreams are frozen in the night.
Whispers echo, soft and low,
Carried by the winter's snow.

Frosted branches, delicate lace,
Time stands still in this serene space.
Footprints fade as if to say,
Winter's magic drifts away.

Chill in the air, a breath of peace,
In this stillness, burdens cease.
Softly wrapped in nature's thread,
Winter's song, so gently spread.

Candlelight through frosted glass,
Moments linger, shadows pass.
Hearts entwined, in quiet cheer,
In whispers of winter, love draws near.

Frosted Dreams on the Edge

Beneath the stars, the cold winds wail,
Dreams take flight, on winter's trail.
Each flake falls, a whispered wish,
In quiet moments, we cherish this.

Glistening fields, a silver sheen,
Frosted whispers, softly glean.
Moonlit paths, where shadows glide,
In this world, our hearts confide.

Every breath, a cloud of mist,
Warmth of hope, in the frost we twist.
Night unfolds with twinkling sights,
Dreams aglow in the tranquil nights.

The edge of darkness, softly tamed,
Where frost and dreams, forever claimed.
A gentle pull, the night weaves tight,
In frosted dreams, we find the light.

Silently we roam, beneath the gaze,
Of winter's spell, in this frozen maze.
Together we chase the morning's gleam,
In frosted dreams, we dare to dream.

Twilight Gleam on Frosty Fields

Twilight casts its gentle glow,
On icy fields where chill winds blow.
A silvery sheen, the world transformed,\nIn winter's arms, our hearts warmed.

Stars awaken in the night sky,
As the day whispers its soft goodbye.
Frosted whispers fill the air,
In twilight's gleam, we find our prayer.

Crystals shimmer like tiny gems,
Upon the earth, nature's diadems.
Each breath taken, a dance of frost,
In this moment, we feel no cost.

Under the moon's tender embrace,
We wander free in this enchanted place.
The beauty speaks in silent tones,
In frosty fields, our spirits moans.

Here we stand, hand in hand,
Lost in wonder, like grains of sand.
Twilight's glow, a fleeting balm,
In frosty fields, our souls grow calm.

Silence Beneath the Flurries

As flurries fall, the world grows still,
A whispered hush upon the hill.
Snowflakes dance in playful spree,
In silence deep, our hearts roam free.

Nestled close, the fire glows,
In shadowed corners, warmth bestows.
Each flake a story, soft and light,
Wrapped in dreams, we hold on tight.

Branches bow under winter's weight,
Nature pauses, as if to wait.
In this calm, we find our way,
Embracing peace at the end of day.

Footprints vanish, lost in time,
Echo of laughter, a tender chime.
Silence holds us, strong and true,
Beneath the flurries, me and you.

With every breath, the stillness reigns,
Carving moments in snowy plains.
In the quiet, love's light shines,
In the silence, our heart defines.

Lights and Shadows of a Frozen Dream

In the quiet of the night,
Stars flicker, skies ignite.
Whispers dance on icy winds,
Dreams unfold as silence begins.

Moonbeams cast a silver glow,
Painting paths where frost can go.
Shadows play in midnight's sway,
Guiding thoughts that drift away.

A glimmer here, a shadow there,
In the heart, dreams lay bare.
Frozen moments, lost in time,
Echoes ring in perfect rhyme.

Through the chill, a fire ignites,
Guiding souls on winter nights.
Dreamers wander, hearts intune,
Chasing tales beneath the moon.

In this realm where dreams are spun,
Lights and shadows, both are one.
Frozen whispers, timeless schemes,
Embrace the magic of our dreams.

Frost's Gentle Touch on Time's Canvas

Frost adorns each morning light,
Painting days in purest white.
Delicate strokes on time's embrace,
Nature's art reveals her grace.

Leaves shiver under winter's spell,
Each branch tells a story well.
In stillness, time begins to pause,
Embraced by winter's subtle laws.

Gentle touch upon the ground,
Hush of silence all around.
Memory captured in icy breath,
Life's beauty whispers of its death.

Every flake a tale to share,
Woven softly in the air.
Time walks slow, in moments freeze,
Frost's embrace, a tranquil tease.

In glistening fields of frosted dreams,
Life flows on in silver streams.
Canvas stretched, yet still it thrives,
With frozen art, our spirit strives.

The Breath of Winter's Reflection

In the breath of winter's chill,
Nature pauses, calm and still.
Mirrored lakes reflect the sky,
A world where dreams and stillness lie.

Every breath, a fading mist,
Moments flow, too sweet to kiss.
Silent echoes, whispers bound,
In the frost, our hearts are found.

Time unravels, crisp and clear,
Winter's voice, soft and near.
As shadows dance beneath the trees,
We are wrapped in winter's tease.

Each reflection tells a tale,
Of lost journeys, winds that sail.
In the silence, we connect,
With the breath of winter's effect.

A gentle sigh, a fleeting glance,
In this realm, we take a chance.
Winter's breath, a soft caress,
In its depths, we find our rest.

Enchanted Twilights Wrapped in Ice

Twilight wraps the world in blue,
Stars awaken, bright and true.
In the hush of evening's glow,
Whispers of the night unfold slow.

Glowing crystals, softly gleam,
Echoing the day's lost theme.
The sky becomes a painted sheet,
Where dreams and night gently meet.

Frosty breaths adorn the air,
Magic lingers everywhere.
In this chill, our spirits rise,
Lost in the enchanted skies.

Every moment, crystal clear,
In the twilight, nothing's near.
Wrapped in ice, yet hearts can burn,
For the warmth in dreams we yearn.

Leave behind the noisy day,
In this stillness, shadows play.
Enchanted twilights, fierce and nice,
We are bound in winter's ice.

Breath of Winter in Stillness

In the hush of the morning light,
Snowflakes whisper, soft and white.
Branches cradle the quiet air,
Nature pauses, a tranquil prayer.

Frost kisses the world, a delicate touch,
Time suspends, feeling like such.
Each breath of icy wind sings low,
Winter's beauty, a peaceful glow.

Footprints scatter on soft white ground,
A fleeting mark, but beauty found.
The silence thickens, dense and deep,
In winter's arms, the earth does sleep.

Illuminated Frost Under Gentle Stars

Stars twinkle in the velvet night,
Frost glimmers with a pearly light.
The world transforms under the glow,
A fairy tale in whispers slow.

Each breath is cloud, a crystal mist,
In this scene, nothing is missed.
Soft echoes of winter's soft embrace,
Beneath the stars, we find our place.

Glistening shadows dance on the ground,
Nature's symphony, a magic sound.
Under gentle skies, we dream anew,
In the cold, our hearts feel true.

Horizon Wrapped in Icy Splendor

The horizon glows with frosty grace,
A world adorned, a stunning place.
Mountains wear their icy crowns,
In serene silence, the earth abounds.

Clouds drift by, in soft embrace,
Painting dreams in a timeless space.
The air is crisp, each moment pure,
In winter's grasp, we feel secure.

Waves of snow glisten on the rise,
A tranquil canvas 'neath vast skies.
Wrapped in splendor, cold and bright,
We find our solace in winter's light.

A Canvas of White Beneath Indigo Skies

Beneath the dome of indigo hue,
A canvas spreads, fresh and new.
White drapes over fields and trees,
A masterpiece that stirs the breeze.

Each flake a brushstroke, nothing less,
Creating wonders in winter's dress.
The earth awakes with a frosty cheer,
In quiet moments, everything's clear.

Footprints crunch in the powdery snow,
Each mark a secret, tales to show.
A serene wilderness, vast and wide,
In this stillness, we find our stride.

Echoes of a Frozen Dawn

Whispers twirl in crisp, cold air,
Frosted branches, a silvery flare.
Sunlight creeps through icy mist,
Nature's beauty, not to be missed.

Silent shadows dance and play,
As night surrenders to a new day.
Footprints trace where dreams have flown,
In the stillness, life is shown.

Morning's breath, a gentle sigh,
Snowflakes weave like stars on high.
Each echo holds a story told,
Of wonder wrapped in threads of gold.

The world awakens, heart aglow,
With whispers of warmth in the snow.
Magic woven through the dawn,
In frozen dreams, we linger on.

Moments twinkle, time slips by,
In the hush beneath the sky.
Echoes linger, soft and clear,
In the dawn's embrace, we draw near.

The Hearth's Warm Gaze

Fires crackle with stories old,
As flames dance and embers scold.
The hearth's glow, a tender light,
Wraps the room in a warm delight.

Comfort rests upon the floor,
With every heartbeat, we explore.
Laughter echoes, a cherished sound,
In this haven, love is found.

Sweet aromas fill the air,
Kindred spirits gather near.
Tales shared 'neath the flickering glow,
Memory stitched in every flow.

Outside, the winter winds may roar,
But here, we find an open door.
In this space, always embraced,
Our hearts and warmth forever traced.

Night descends, candles flicker,
In this glow, our lives grow thicker.
From hearth to heart, we reach the skies,
In each smile, love never dies.

Beneath the Winter's Shroud

Veils of snow, so softly laid,
Blanket dreams, tranquil and staid.
Nature whispers in hues of white,
Holding secrets, pure and bright.

Creatures pause in silent grace,
Hidden beneath this wintry space.
Tracks meander, a path so rare,
Leading spirits through crisp air.

The world revolves, a frozen dance,
Each gust of wind a fleeting chance.
To find solace in gentle cold,
Where stories of old are retold.

Stars peer down, watchful and proud,
Shimmering through the winter's shroud.
A silver hush, a tranquil night,
Cloaked in darkness, wrapped in light.

As dawn's first blush touches the frost,
We rise anew, never truly lost.
Beneath the shroud, we find our way,
Emerging bright, come what may.

Sled Tracks to Infinity

Gliding down the slopes so free,
Wind whispers songs just for me.
Each sled track a fleeting dream,
Carving paths through silver gleam.

Laughter rings in the crisp night air,
With every climb, we shed our care.
Bounding forth, spirits soar high,
In these moments, we touch the sky.

The thrill ignites, a joyous spark,
Under starlight, we leave our mark.
With every turn, we ride the night,
In search of trails, pure delight.

The moon smiles down, a guiding light,
Carving joys in the quiet night.
Tracks blend in a tapestry wide,
Infinite wonders, as we glide.

Chasing dreams through the snowy glow,
In each heartbeat, our laughter flows.
Sled tracks vanish, yet still they stay,
Reminders of love in winter's play.

Beyond the Blushing Horizon

Golden rays kiss the dawn,
Birds take flight to greet the morn.
Clouds blush soft, a tender hue,
Whispers of dreams that feel so true.

Mountains stand in silent grace,
Holding secrets, time won't erase.
Paths unwinding, hearts that roam,
Underneath the sky, we find our home.

Every shadow tells a tale,
Of hopes and fears, both frail and pale.
As light dances on the sea,
We chase the moments, wild and free.

Waves of color brush the land,
Painting memories, hand in hand.
In this place, our souls ignite,
Beyond the blushing, pure delight.

Glistening Echoes of the Past

Through the fog, a whisper calls,
As evening shadows softly fall.
Memories glisten like the dew,
Echoes of what we once knew.

Paths we wandered, side by side,
In laughter shared, our hearts confide.
Each step taken stitched with light,
Binding us through day and night.

Reflections dance upon the stream,
In every corner, a forgotten dream.
The stars above hum old refrains,
In silent woods and whispered plains.

Turn the page, the stories weave,
A tapestry we won't believe.
Golden threads of joy and strife,
Glistening echoes, the pulse of life.

Secrets Wrapped in Frost

Morning comes, a veil of white,
Secrets wrapped in frosty light.
Each crystal flake a story holds,
Of whispered dreams and nights so cold.

Trees adorned in icy lace,
Nature's art, a timeless grace.
Footsteps crunch on paths anew,
In this world.
I walk with you.

Frozen whispers fill the air,
In the stillness, hearts lay bare.
Underneath the frost's embrace,
Lies the warmth of hope's sweet face.

Hidden truths beneath the chill,
Yearning hearts, a quiet thrill.
As twilight falls, the secrets gleam,
Wrapped in frost, they softly dream.

The Edge of a Whispering Snowdrift

At the edge of night, we find,
Snowdrifts whisper, soft and kind.
Moonlight glows on blankets white,
Cradling dreams in the quiet night.

Stars above like diamonds shine,
Casting paths where hearts align.
Each flake falls, a gentle sigh,
Carrying wishes to the sky.

Through the woods, the shadows play,
Whispers linger, soft ballet.
Every breath, a spark of light,
In the calm, we chase the night.

Together near the snow's embrace,
Time suspended, a sacred space.
In that stillness, we shall drift,
At the edge, our spirits lift.

Frozen Realms of Twilight's Glow

In twilight's grasp the snowflakes fall,
A shimmering veil, a silent call.
The world adorned in crystals bright,
Beneath the stars, a tranquil night.

Whispers of frost in the gentle breeze,
Nature sleeps, at ease with the freeze.
The moonlight dances on icicles clear,
Painting dreams where shadows appear.

A silver mist drapes over the pines,
Each branch a canvas where stillness shines.
Frozen realms in the dusk's embrace,
Serene reflections in time and space.

Colors dim as the day grows old,
Stories of winters through ages told.
A hush falls deep, the world held tight,
In frozen slumber, wrapped in light.

As night deepens, the visions wane,
In twilight's glow, we lose the pain.
Frozen realms forever hold,
The magic written in whispers bold.

Palette of Winter's Quiet Palette

Winter's canvas, soft and wide,
Brushstrokes gentle, with dreams inside.
Whites and blues in a subtle flow,
A quiet scene, a melting snow.

Each flake unique, a fleeting art,
Nature's love in every part.
Silent echoes of a world embraced,
By winter's charm, forever traced.

Footprints whisper on untouched ground,
In the palette where hush is found.
A sparkling hush, the world at rest,
In winter's arms, we are blessed.

The stillness deepens, shadows play,
Colors blend as night meets day.
A tranquil heart, a peaceful mind,
In this palette, solace we find.

Every brush dipped in silver light,
Crafts a magic in frosty night.
The palette glows in whispers sweet,
Where winter's wonder and stillness meet.

An Arctic Spell at Day's End

Day's end whispers soft and low,
An arctic spell begins to show.
With hues of orange and fading pink,
The icy realms start to blink.

Mountains crowned in frost's embrace,
Silhouettes in a glowing lace.
The horizon merges with the sky,
As day bids farewell, we sigh.

Every breath comes in misty puffs,
Nature's wonder, it never thuffs.
Stars emerge in a velvet sea,
As shadows weave a tapestry.

The calm night wraps the world so tight,
In this spell, everything feels right.
An arctic charm, a soothing balm,
In day's end stillness, hearts feel calm.

Moments linger, as time suspends,
Caught in the magic that winter lends.
An arctic spell, soft and grand,
As night descends on this frostbit land.

When Time Pauses in the Chill

In winter's breath, the stillness grows,
When time pauses in the chill it knows.
Each moment stretches, long and deep,
While nature sings her lullaby, we sleep.

Frost-kissed windows frame the scene,
Of quietude, a tranquil sheen.
The world outside, a crystal dream,
Where every breath is a soft-themed stream.

Moments wrapped in white embrace,
In this stillness, we find our place.
Time takes a breath, a gentle sigh,
In chilled whispers where echoes lie.

Candles flicker, casting warm light,
Creating magic in the night.
In the chill, our hearts ignite,
As time pauses, holding tight.

Wrapped in blankets, stories unfold,
While outside, the snowflakes dance bold.
In winter's grasp, we find our thrills,
When time pauses in the chill.

A Pathway Through the Icy Mists

Through the mist where shadows play,
I wander lost in white display.
Footfalls whisper on the frost,
In this realm, I find my cost.

Silent trees, their branches bare,
Wrapped in ice, they stand and stare.
Every breath is crystal clear,
Nature's song, a gentle cheer.

In the distance, echoes call,
As I trace the ancient wall.
Winding paths, like dreams, unfold,
Misty tales of winter told.

Softly glimmers moon above,
Guiding me with silver love.
In this ever-frozen land,
A hidden beauty, vast and grand.

As I tread this quiet way,
Magic grows with light of day.
Each moment, a breath of peace,
In the mists, my thoughts release.

Frost-Laden Chronicles Under Moon's Watch

Beneath the glow of silver light,
Frosted tales unfold at night.
Whispers carried on the breeze,
Chronicles of chill and trees.

Crystals dance on blades of grass,
Time slows down as shadows pass.
Every star a tale to spin,
Lost in dreams, the night begins.

The moon, a guardian so wise,
Sees the world through frost-kissed eyes.
In this quiet, peace resides,
Where thoughts linger and hope hides.

Through the night, the stories blend,
Whispers of souls, both lost and penned.
I stand alone, yet not alone,
In this realm, my heart has grown.

A tapestry of frozen sights,
Weaving warmth into cold nights.
Under moon's watch, fear dissolves,
And within, the heart resolves.

Serenity Found in Frosted Corners

In frosted corners, silence blooms,
Whispers echo through the rooms.
A gentle hush wraps 'round the night,
Filling hearts with pure delight.

Snowflakes drift like whispered prayers,
Draping dreams in frozen layers.
Each flake tells a story told,
Of warmth beneath the bitter cold.

Candles flicker, shadows play,
As warmth and light begin to sway.
In every nook, a treasure lies,
Serenity in quiet sighs.

Through the glass, a world transformed,
In winter's grip, our hearts are warmed.
Frosted corners hold their grace,
Wrapped in love's soft, sweet embrace.

With every dawn, new light shall break,
Guiding paths where dreams awake.
In frosted corners, peace is found,
A gentle heartbeat, soft and round.

A Reverie in Winter's Silken Breath

In winter's breath, a dream awakes,
Soft as silk, the silence makes.
Gentle whispers fill the air,
Carried on the frosty flare.

Snowflakes twirl in graceful flight,
Dancing under pale moonlight.
Every moment, life anew,
A reverie of shades and hue.

Time stands still in this embrace,
Painted white, the world finds grace.
With every breath, a chance to feel,
Winter's secrets softly heal.

Fields of white stretch far and wide,
In this stillness, hearts confide.
Every sigh, a tale unspun,
In winter's web, we all are one.

As dawn approaches, shadows fade,
Whispers linger, memories made.
In winter's breath, we find our way,
A reverie that shall not sway.

Whistling Winds Through Bare Trees

Whistling winds through bare trees,
Whispers of winter's breath.
Branches sway, their dance a tease,
Echoes of nature's death.

Leaves have fallen, ground is bare,
Frost-kissed twigs reach for the sky.
Silence drapes the frozen air,
While shadows linger, shy.

Underneath the starlit sky,
Moonlight filters through the night.
Rustling sounds like a soft sigh,
Nature holds its breath in fright.

Hushed moments, calm and deep,
Nighttime's veil a gentle cloak.
In the stillness, dreams do creep,
Awakening with each spoke.

Whistling winds, a haunting call,
Reminding me of days long past.
Through the woods I hear them all,
Nature's song, forever cast.

Reflections on a Frozen Lake

Reflections dance on frozen lake,
Mirrored skies and whispered dreams.
Silvery sheen, a tranquil ache,
Captured light in silken seams.

Ice-bound edges, fragile glow,
Cracked and creased, a silent sigh.
Beneath the surface, currents flow,
Hidden tales, too deep to pry.

Birds glide above, in graceful arcs,
Leaving ripples, soft and small.
Nature's choir, with chirps like sparks,
Serenades the nightfall's call.

Footsteps crunch on winter's crust,
Each step echoes in the calm.
Moments frozen, held in trust,
Nature's melody, a balm.

Reflections on this frozen space,
Whispers of the seasons blend.
A canvas of time, a sacred place,
Where earth and sky gently mend.

Dreams Adrift in Crystal Silence

Dreams adrift in crystal silence,
Woven threads of starlit night.
In the void, whispers of defiance,
Echoing without a light.

Glistening snowflakes softly fall,
Crystals catch the moon's embrace.
In this realm, I hear the call,
Of a world in tranquil grace.

Every breath a snowy sigh,
Frozen moments captured still.
Winds carry dreams that drift and fly,
Spirits dance upon the chill.

Thoughts like flurries, light and free,
Twisting in the midnight air.
In this vast eternity,
Hope is birthed from whispered prayer.

Dreams adrift, I wander far,
In the silence, fears release.
Finding solace in the star,
Where all hearts can find their peace.

Stardust and Icicles

Stardust and icicles collide,
Glistening gems in the frosted air.
Winter's breath in whispers wide,
Dreams suspended, quite rare.

Icicles hanging, sharp yet clear,
Fractured light, a crystal song.
Each droplet echoes what we hold dear,
In this world where we belong.

Stars twinkle in the endless night,
Softly guiding, lighting the way.
Whispers weave through the icy bite,
Promises of dawn's new day.

Beneath the moon's celestial glow,
Hearts entwined in nature's art.
In the stillness, feelings flow,
Uniting every distant heart.

Stardust mingles with the chill,
Memory lingers in the freeze.
In this magic, time stands still,
Where dreams and nature find their ease.

The Glistening Edge of Dusk

The day bows low with grace,
As shadows blend with light.
Whispers of the night embrace,
In hues of soft twilight.

Chill air carries scents of pine,
While stars begin to wink.
The world slips into a line,
Between the dark and pink.

A breeze stirs thoughts unspun,
Each heartbeat marks the hour.
Dreams awaken, one by one,
Beneath the ghostly power.

On hills where secrets seep,
The stories come alive.
In silence, beauty sleeps,
As nature starts to thrive.

The moon draws forth our gaze,
In velvet's softest loom.
A canvas framed in haze,
Where shadows softly bloom.

Shimmering Veil of White

A blanket folds the earth anew,
In gentle grace, it lies.
Each flake a crystal, pure and true,
Beneath the silver skies.

Footsteps crunch on frosty ground,
As laughter fills the air.
In every corner, joy is found,
As winter's magic's rare.

Branches wear a frosted crown,
With diamonds in their hair.
The world transformed, no hints of brown,
In beauty beyond compare.

The sun peeks through the veil of white,
With golden warmth to see.
In every heart, a spark of light,
As nature's harmony.

At dusk, the shadows softly grow,
Enveloping the land.
In winter's hush, a gentle glow,
A moment, simply grand.

Secrets Beneath the Frozen Glaze

Layers hide the earth's embrace,
In stillness wrapped in white.
Beneath the crust, a soft, warm space,
Where secrets hover light.

With every step, the echoes call,
Of whispers long since lost.
In frozen realms, we feel them all,
No matter what the cost.

The world holds its breath to hear,
The tales of those who tread.
In silence, truth can's crystal clear,
As night paints all in red.

A tapestry of icy dreams,
Woven in the night.
Life dances in silent seams,
In shadows, soft and bright.

As morning breaks, the veil will lift,
Revealing all we seek.
Yet in the freeze, a precious gift,
Of secrets still unique.

A Tapestry of Glimmering Chill

Threads of frost weave through the air,
Creates a vision rare.
As dawn breaks clear and fair,
Each moment's stripped of care.

The landscape dressed in sheer delight,
A wonder in the morn.
With every glint, the sun ignites,
A world forever born.

In whispers soft, the cold invites,
To dance in sparkling glow.
The chill caresses, softly bites,
And lets warm currents flow.

Fragments of wonder twist and turn,
In every path we trace.
A tapestry we yearn to learn,
As winter's sweet embrace.

With each exhale, we paint a scene,
Of beauty intertwined.
In icy veins, the world convenes,
Where hearts and dreams align.

The Chill of Dawn's Embrace

Whispers of the morning breeze,
Softly kiss the sleepy trees.
A blush of light begins to glow,
As shadows dance, the night must go.

With every breath, a fragile chill,
The world awakens, calm and still.
In pastel hues, the sky rebirths,
Embracing all with gentle mirth.

The dew drops cling on blades of grass,
Like jeweled hopes that dare to pass.
Birds begin their morning song,
A chorus sweet, where hearts belong.

Beneath the arches of soft dawn,
The sleepy stars begin to yawn.
Nature's canvas, painted bright,
Revealing magic in the light.

In stillness found, a moment stays,
As day unfolds in golden rays.
The chill of dawn, a tender lace,
Wraps the world in a warm embrace.

Icicles Draped in Moonlight

Underneath the moon's soft glow,
Icicles glitter, row by row.
Hanging like tears from eaves above,
Nature crafting art in love.

Chilled breaths hang in frosty air,
The night is quiet, rich, and rare.
Silver beams reflect the light,
Casting dreams into the night.

Each icicle a crystal spear,
Whispering secrets to the ear.
A frozen dance, a silent call,
Nature's beauty for us all.

Shadows play on the frozen ground,
As whispers of winter all around.
Wrapped in blankets, hearts reside,
In the peace where dreams abide.

With every sparkle, magic weaves,
In the stillness, our heart believes.
Icicles glisten, a silver sight,
In the embrace of the moon's light.

Frosted Tapestry at Dusk

As daylight fades, a curtain falls,
Draped in frost, the evening calls.
A tapestry of silver threads,
Weaves a tale where beauty spreads.

Mountains wear their winter coat,
Echoing whispers as stars emote.
Crystals twinkle in twilight's hand,
Crafting magic across the land.

The trees stand tall, a frosted choir,
Singing softly, a gentle fire.
In hushed tones, the night descends,
As daylight wanes, and silence bends.

In this realm where shadows play,
A world transformed, a grand ballet.
Each step wrapped in winter's grace,
Embracing night in a warm embrace.

With every breath, the chill unfolds,
A cozy spell as night enfolds.
Amidst the sparkles, dreams ignite,
In the frosted tapestry of night.

Glimmers in the Crystal Veil

In a world serene and bright,
Glimmers dance in soft moonlight.
A crystal veil wraps all in white,
Whispers of magic, pure delight.

Snowflakes falling, one by one,
Kissing earth like a gentle drum.
Each flake unique, a fleeting art,
Painting landscapes that touch the heart.

Beneath the branches, shadows glide,
Where laughter echoes, dreams abide.
Every twinkle a fleeting song,
As winter weaves where hearts belong.

With frosted breaths, the night unfolds,
A story of warmth amidst the cold.
Glimmers shine where hopes prevail,
In the beauty of the crystal veil.

So let us gather, side by side,
Embrace the magic, let it guide.
For in this world, where dreams unveil,
We find the joy in the crystal veil.

When Shadows Dance on Ice

The moonlight gleams on frozen streams,
Whispers of night weave silent dreams.
Figures glide with grace divine,
In a world where star and shadow intertwine.

Beneath the trees, the shadows play,
Dancing lights in the frost's ballet.
Echoes of laughter trace the ground,
In this realm where magic's found.

Cool winds weave through the frozen air,
A symphony rare, radiating care.
Each spin and twirl, a tale of old,
In whispers of winter, enchantments unfold.

Silhouettes flicker, brief and bright,
In the hush of the calm, the heart takes flight.
As shadows dance, we lose all sense,
Of time and space, in this vast expanse.

So let the ice cradle every sigh,
For in this moment, we softly fly.
With shadows as guides, we find our way,
In the magic found at the end of day.

In the Stillness of the Snowfall

A blanket white on the world so still,
Whispers of winter upon the hill.
Snowflakes drift like gentle dreams,
Clad in silence, nature beams.

The trees stand tall, adorned in lace,
Each bough a canvas, a timeless grace.
Footsteps muffled in soft embrace,
In the stillness, we find our place.

Breath hangs frozen, a fleeting sigh,
Under the canvas of a pale sky.
Stars blink softly down to see,
The beauty born from tranquility.

Laughter echoes in the frosty glow,
As children rejoice in the falling snow.
Warmth in hearts, we gather near,
In the stillness, love draws near.

So let us wander through this dream,
In the hush, where time does seem.
To pause and breathe in this pure delight,
In the stillness of the snowy night.

Crystalline Echoes at Twilight

The sun bows low, a tender hue,
As twilight whispers, soft and true.
Crystalline echoes fill the air,
Mirrored moments, a beauty rare.

From golden dawn to violet's kiss,
Each fleeting second, a brush of bliss.
Nature's orchestra begins to play,
As light and shadow dance and sway.

Echoes shimmer on the frost-kissed ground,
In the twilight, magic is found.
A tapestry woven, silver and blue,
As day softly waves its last adieu.

The stars awaken, one by one,
In the embrace of a setting sun.
Hope takes flight on crystalline wings,
In twilight's arms, our spirit sings.

So let the night weave dreams so bright,
In crystalline echoes, find your light.
For in this moment, we glimpse the divine,
In the twilight's glow, our hearts align.

Fragments of Light in Frost

In the early dawn, a spark unfolds,
As frost weaves magic in silvery molds.
Each blade of grass, a crystal bright,
Holds fragments of morning's gentle light.

The air is still, the world in slumber,
As sunlight kisses the frost in wonder.
Glimmers and glows, a soft embrace,
Nature awakens with vibrant grace.

Footprints trail where dreams reside,
In the canvas of winter, we laugh and glide.
Frosty breath dances in the morning sun,
Fragments of joy as a new day's begun.

The trees shimmer with a radiant sheen,
In the heart of winter, beauty unseen.
We chase the light through the fields of white,
In a world sprinkled with pure delight.

So let us gather these moments dear,
In fragments of light, our path is clear.
In the frost's embrace, we find our way,
In the whispers of dawn, we welcome the day.

Tranquil Horizons of Gleaming White

The snow drapes softly on the ground,
A quiet blanket, pure and profound.
Footprints crunch with a gentle sound,
In this stillness, peace is found.

Trees stand tall, their branches bare,
Whispers of wind, a cool, crisp air.
In the distance, mountains share,
A beauty that leaves souls laid bare.

Colors fade into shades of gray,
As twilight beckons, ending the day.
Stars awaken, ready to play,
In tranquil nights, dreams find their way.

Each breath taken, a frosty sigh,
Under the vast, starry sky.
Hope lingers as night drifts by,
A moment held, we cannot deny.

In the stillness, time stands still,
Nature rests, a sacred thrill.
Hearts align with a gentle will,
In tranquil horizons, we find our fill.

Enchanted by the Arctic Breeze

Gentle whispers through the pines,
An Arctic breath, where magic shines.
The air is crisp, with hidden signs,
Of beauty found, where nature entwines.

Snowflakes dance in shimmering light,
Creating wonders, pure delight.
A world transformed, so calm and bright,
As day fades into the peaceful night.

Beyond the hills, the auroras sway,
Colors of dreams in bright ballet.
Mother Nature's grand display,
In this magic, we long to stay.

The silence holds a timeless lore,
With every gust, it calls for more.
In the heart, we find our core,
Enchanted by the breeze we explore.

A moment shared beneath the stars,
Far from chaos, near and far.
In the stillness, we heal our scars,
Embracing the peace, like a shining star.

Silk of Frost on Nature's Canvas

Dewdrops glisten like pearls of grace,
Covering the world in a soft embrace.
Frost paints patterns, a delicate lace,
Nature's canvas, a perfect space.

Whispers of winter in every breath,
Silent echoes of life and death.
Every tree stands proud, a wreath,
Of frost and time, a sacred sheath.

The sun peeks gently, warming the cold,
Lights up stories that have been told.
In hues of silver, bright and bold,
Nature's beauty, a sight to behold.

With each step, the world unfolds,
A tapestry woven of dreams and gold.
Silken frost, its magic consoles,
In these moments, the heart extols.

Savor the chill, embrace the charm,
Let nature's wonders weave and disarm.
In frosty spells, find peace and calm,
Wrapped in the silk, forever warm.

The Radiance of Winter Sunsets

As day retreats, the sky ignites,
With hues of orange, reds, and lights.
Winter's breath in tranquil sights,
Painting dreams on cold, clear nights.

Golden rays touch the snowy ground,
A fleeting moment, beauty unbound.
In the stillness, the world is crowned,
As twilight whispers, softly profound.

Crisp air carries the scent of pine,
With each heartbeat, stars align.
A dance of colors, simply divine,
In this radiance, our dreams entwine.

The horizon glows with fading light,
Kissing day goodbye, igniting night.
With every shadow, a spark ignites,
In winter's arms, everything feels right.

Hold the moment, let it remain,
In the silence, we find no pain.
As the stars emerge, our hearts explain,
In the radiance, love will sustain.

Hoarfrost's Gentle Caress

Whispers of dawn, a soft embrace,
Nature unveils her frosty lace.
Each blade of grass a crystal spear,
Hoarfrost sings, winter is here.

Trees adorned in shimmering white,
Glisten gently in morning light.
A silent world, so calm and still,
Nature's beauty, hearts to fill.

Footsteps crunch on icy ground,
In this magic, joy is found.
The air is crisp, a breath of peace,
A moment's pause, a sweet release.

Children's laughter fills the air,
Snowflakes dance with playful flair.
With every smile, the chill departs,
Warmth ignites in open hearts.

Hoarfrost's touch, a fleeting muse,
In its splendor, we won't refuse.
A gentle caress, nature's art,
In winter's grasp, we play our part.

In the Realm of Silvered Light

Silvery beams break through the dawn,
Softly lifting shadows drawn.
A tranquil hush enfolds the ground,
In this realm, pure peace is found.

Glistening paths reflect the skies,
Whispers of dreams in each surprise.
Frosted branches, a frozen spell,
Entranced by beauty, all is well.

Each step taken feels divine,
As the world shimmers, all align.
In this moment, time stands still,
The heart is hushed, the mind can thrill.

A dance of light, a fleeting ghost,
In winter's grace, we cherish most.
The silver glow, a sacred art,
Illuminates the beating heart.

Through veils of ice, we wander free,
Bound by nature's mystery.
In the realm of silvered light,
We find our truth in pure delight.

A Canvas of Icy Serenity

Frozen lakes in serene repose,
Nature whispers, the cold wind blows.
A canvas white, the world so bright,
Icy beauty, a pure delight.

Snowflakes twirl in a gentle dance,
Each one unique, a fleeting chance.
Patterns form on windowpanes,
Artistry where silence reigns.

Peace wrapped tight in winter's fold,
Stories of warmth yet untold.
In the soft glow of twilight's hue,
We gather close, our spirits anew.

A tranquil space, a sacred trust,
Beneath the frost, the earth is hushed.
In every flake, a dream alive,
In icy serenity, we thrive.

A moment captured, time holds still,
A world transformed by winter's will.
A canvas hung in nature's art,
Uniting us, heart to heart.

Chasing Shadows in a Winter Wonderland

Footprints trace a winding way,
Through the hush of winter's play.
Chasing shadows, laughter rings,
In this realm, our spirit sings.

Snow-draped hills invite the thrill,
A joy that only children fill.
Sleds and joy, a racing dream,
In a world wrapped in silver gleam.

Whirling winds, the breath of frost,
In this wonderland, we are lost.
Each snowflake whispers soft and low,
Secrets of magic buried in snow.

The sky fades soft in hues of gray,
As the sun bids the light to sway.
Yet in the shadows, we find delight,
In winter's wonder, pure and bright.

Chasing shadows, hearts entwine,
In the cold, our warmth will shine.
In this wonderland we roam,
Together, we find our way back home.

Whispers of Frosted Dawn

In the hush of morning light,
Frosted petals gleam and shine,
Nature whispers soft and bright,
Wrapped in winter's tender vine.

Trees stand still, their branches bare,
Draped in white like ancient lace,
Every breath hangs in the air,
A tranquil moment we embrace.

Footsteps crunch on snowy ground,
Echoes dance in the stillness,
Peaceful silence all around,
A world kissed by nature's chillness.

Birds return with songs so sweet,
Notes flow gently, soft and low,
In this dawn, our hearts compete,
Finding warmth in winter's glow.

As the sun begins to rise,
Colors paint the morning sky,
Frosted whispers, soft goodbyes,
In the dawn, we learn to fly.

Celestial Blankets of Winter

Blankets white on slumbering earth,
Peace enfolds each sleeping space,
Stars above bring quiet mirth,
In night's arms, we find our grace.

Crystalline flakes drift and swirl,
Whirling dancers from the skies,
Their descent a soft, sweet pearl,
Whispers echo, truth defies.

Every branch and every stone,
Holds the magic of the night,
In a world so overgrown,
Winter's beauty shines so bright.

Through the trees, the moonlight streams,
Casting shadows long and lean,
In this quiet, wrapped in dreams,
Life is pure, and hearts are clean.

Morning breaks, the frost will fade,
But the memories will remain,
In the chill, we've gently played,
Winter's brush, a soft refrain.

Embrace of the Icy Realm

Winds do whisper through the pines,
Cool caress upon the skin,
Nature weaves her frosty lines,
In her grasp, we feel akin.

Frozen streams that glisten bright,
Mirror skies of azure hue,
In the day and through the night,
Life finds beauty, fresh and new.

Mountains crowned with purest snow,
Guardians of the silent night,
Each step crunches, soft and slow,
In their presence, hearts take flight.

Fog rolls in with muted grace,
A delicate, ghostly shroud,
In this stillness, we can trace,
The peace found in winter's crowd.

Every flake, a tale to tell,
Each moment etched, here to claimed,
In this realm where whispers dwell,
We lose ourselves, forever framed.

Frosted Dreams and Chilled Whispers

Crystalline dreams beneath our feet,
Shadows stretch as daylight fades,
In this hush, the world's discreet,
Whispers form in winter glades.

Stars like diamonds fill the night,
Mirroring the icy ground,
In their glow, we find our light,
Silence all around us sounds.

Frosted branches, breath of air,
Each exhale a lingering mist,
Nature's canvas, rich and rare,
Moments caught that can't be missed.

Through the chill, a fire burns,
Warmth within our hearts remains,
In this dance, the heart still yearns,
Echoed softly in the rains.

Every winter's tale unfolds,
In the tapestry of time,
Frosted dreams, and whispers bold,
In a world where love will rhyme.

Dreaming in a Winter's Embrace

Whispers wrap in snowy folds,
A tranquil hush, as night unfolds.
Stars twinkle through a silver sheen,
In dreams of warmth, we find the serene.

Frosted windows, lace designs,
Each breath a cloud, as winter signs.
The world is still, a breath held tight,
In winter's arms, we find the light.

Snowflakes dance in ghostly light,
Carrying wishes through the night.
Together we knit warmth from cold,
Embracing dreams, our hearts unfold.

Candles flicker, shadows play,
As we drift far from the day.
Enveloped in a glowing haze,
Dreaming softly through the maze.

Morning beckons, softly calls,
Winter's breath as daylight falls.
In our hearts, the warmth remains,
A winter's embrace, love retains.

Veils of Ice and Crystal Light

Veils of ice adorn the trees,
Glistening bright in winter's breeze.
Nature crafts with careful hands,
A sparkling world, where magic stands.

Crystal shards catch morning's glow,
Reflecting dreams that gently flow.
Each step whispers beneath the sky,
As wonder paints the earth nearby.

Beneath the sun, the frost does melt,
But memories of winter felt.
In silence, we savor the sight,
Of veils adorned in crystal light.

Rivers glide beneath the frost,
In nature's hold, we're never lost.
Surrounded by this beauty rare,
Our hearts find joy in the cold air.

As twilight wraps the day in peace,
Ice-laced dreams will never cease.
In winter's splendor, we delight,
Veils of ice and crystal light.

Whispers of the Frostbitten Breeze

Whispers carried on the night,
The frostbitten breeze takes flight.
Rustling leaves, a shivering sound,
In winter's breath, a calm surrounds.

Moonlight dances on the snow,
Casting shadows, soft and low.
Nature's secrets, softly shared,
In the chill, we're unprepared.

Frosted breaths in silver air,
Together, lost in twilight's glare.
The world a canvas, pure and white,
In whispers of the starlit night.

Cold embraces every lane,
In quietude, we feel the strain.
Yet warmth still flickers in our heart,
As echoes of the night depart.

With every breath, we feel the grace,
Of frostbitten air we embrace.
In its whispers, we find ease,
Together held by winter's breeze.

Evening Glow on Frosted Pines

Evening settles, softly glows,
On frosted pines, a light that knows.
Shadows stretch in golden hue,
As twilight whispers, calm and true.

The sky ignites in shades of gold,
Stories of the day unfold.
Each branch adorned with winter's lace,
The world transformed, a warm embrace.

As night descends, the stars appear,
A canvas bright, enchanting sphere.
In the stillness, hearts entwine,
Beneath the evening glow, divine.

Crispness mingles with the air,
Frosty whispers everywhere.
Yet in the chill, we seek the light,
In enchanted realms of night.

Among the pines, we stand as one,
Chasing dreams until they're spun.
With every breath, we feel the sign,
Of evening glow on frosted pines.

Embracing the Quietude of Winter

Snowflakes fall, a gentle hush,
Winds whisper soft, in twilight's brush.
The world wrapped in a silver sheet,
Each breath a cloud, serene and sweet.

Branches bare, with crystals gleam,
Fires crackle, thoughts drift like dream.
Stillness here, where shadows play,
In winter's arms, we find our way.

The stars peek through the icy veil,
Moonlight dances, a glistening trail.
Footprints fade in the sparkling white,
A moment preserved in the calm of night.

Hot cocoa warms our weary hands,
As cozy echoes fill the lands.
Together we share this tranquil space,
Embracing winter's soft embrace.

In quietude, we find our song,
Nature's chorus, sweet and strong.
In winter's heart, we live in peace,
A time to pause, our joys increase.

The Dance of Frost Under Midnight Skies

Underneath a shroud of stars,
Frost whispers tales from afar.
In the stillness, time slows down,
Nature's beauty wears her crown.

Each breath a mist, a fleeting thought,
Beneath the moon, the cold is sought.
Dance of frost, a swaying glow,
In midnight's arms, we sway and flow.

Crystals form with every sigh,
Glimmers caught in the night's eye.
A symphony of twinkling light,
Wrapped in warmth, we glow so bright.

The world at peace, adorned in white,
We move with grace, lost in delight.
Under winter's spell, we glide,
In frosty dreams, we softly bide.

Let the whispers fill our hearts,
As winter's chill in silence starts.
We find our rhythms, slow and free,
In this dance of frost, just you and me.

Tales from a Glacial Wonderland

In a realm where silence reigns,
Glaciers whisper ancient chains.
Stories carved in ice and stone,
Nature's magic, all alone.

Crystalline wonders, sharp and bright,
Reflect the dawn, a pure delight.
With every step, a tale unfolds,
Frozen secrets waiting, bold.

An icy lake, a mirror clear,
Echoes of laughter, soft and near.
In wonderland, we venture wide,
Through frosted trails, our dreams reside.

The world transformed, a stunning view,
Each moment captured, pure and true.
As shadows lengthen, day departs,
We breathe in tales that melt our hearts.

A glacial wonder, vast and grand,
Together we explore this land.
In whispers sweet, we'll find our place,
Within the tales, we share in grace.

Chasing Glimmers on Frosty Paths

Footprints crunch on frosty ground,
A world where wonders can be found.
Each glimmer sparkles in the light,
Chasing magic through the night.

Beneath our boots, a crackling sound,
Nature's jewels, all around.
In the stillness, our laughter rings,
Awakening the joy it brings.

The path is lined with silvery sheen,
Moments captured, bright and keen.
With every turn, a story blooms,
Unfolding mysteries in the glooms.

As the moonlight dances on the trees,
We wander where the night-time breathes.
In frosty nooks, we lose our way,
Yet find ourselves in the play of sway.

Through the cold, our spirits soar,
Chasing glimmers, we explore.
In winter's grasp, we freely roam,
In frosty paths, we've found our home.

The Call of Frost's Lullaby

In silver whispers, chill winds sing,
A lullaby the cold nights bring.
Each flake that falls, a tender kiss,
Embraced in winter's quiet bliss.

Beneath the moon, the world does sleep,
In frosty dreams, our secrets keep.
As shadows dance on icy streams,
We weave our hopes in frozen dreams.

A crystal veil of shimmering light,
Guiding lost hearts through the night.
With every breath, the silence grows,
In love's deep warmth, the cold wind blows.

The stars above, like jewels rare,
Reflect the dreams we used to share.
In stillness wrapped, we tread so slow,
On paths where only whispers flow.

So hear the call, oh heart so true,
Frost's lullaby will see us through.
In harmony, we'll brave the chill,
Together strong, in winter's thrill.

Memory of a Glistening Trail

Upon the ground, a path we tread,
With memories of words unsaid.
Each step a glimmer, soft and bright,
In winter's glow, we find our light.

The trees stand tall, their branches sway,
While snowflakes dance, a fleeting ballet.
In silence wrapped, our laughter rings,
Echoing joy that winter brings.

The crunch of snow beneath our feet,
A heartbeat found in winter's beat.
With every step, the past awakes,
In glistening trails, our spirit stakes.

Beneath the weight of time's embrace,
We carve our dreams, a sacred space.
A memory etched in frosty air,
A bond that blooms beyond compare.

So let us wander, hand in hand,
Through frosted fields, across the land.
Together we shall leave a trace,
In memory's glow, our timeless grace.

Veil of Frost Between Us

A veil of frost hangs in the air,
Between our hearts, a fragile snare.
Each breath a whisper, soft and clear,
In winter's grip, we draw so near.

The world around us, painted white,
As stars peer down with twinkling light.
Yet in this chill, there stirs a fire,
In every glance, a deep desire.

The icy branches sway and bend,
As if to say this love won't end.
With every flake that falls tonight,
We weave our dreams in silver light.

Though frost may cover what we know,
A warmth within begins to grow.
So come, dear heart, let's brave the cold,
In love's embrace, we find our hold.

Through every winter's chilling sigh,
We'll face the storms and learn to fly.
With every heartbeat, I see you there,
Veil of frost, but love laid bare.

Evening Threads in Arctic Loom

In evening's grasp, the shadows shift,
As threads of dusk in silence drift.
In arctic calm, we find our way,
Through woven dreams of yesterday.

The twilight glows with hues so deep,
As night descends, the world will sleep.
Each star a stitch in night's embrace,
A tapestry of time and space.

The frost below, a canvas bare,
Where whispered secrets fill the air.
We navigate this winter trail,
With courage strong, we will prevail.

With every thread, we spin our tale,
In unity, we shall not fail.
The warmth between us, bittersweet,
In the chill, our hearts still beat.

So weave with me, in night's cool loom,
Together crafting love's sweet bloom.
In evening's fold, we'll find our peace,
A bond that time will not release.

An Ode to the Winter Mirage

In silence deep, the snowflakes fall,
A dreamlike veil, a winter's call.
The world transformed, a canvas white,
Where shadows dance in the soft moonlight.

The air is crisp, a breath divine,
Frosty whispers, a secret sign.
The trees adorned in glittering lace,
Nature's beauty, a warm embrace.

Gentle winds weave through the night,
Carrying tales of pure delight.
Stars above in a velvet sky,
Remind us of joy that will never die.

Each crystal shard, a story told,
Of winter's heart, steadfast and bold.
Embrace the chill, let your spirit soar,
For in this mirage, we seek for more.

The Awakening of the Frozen Day

Awaken now, the slumbering land,
With morning light, so crisp and grand.
Silent forests, creatures hide,
Beneath the frost, nature confides.

The sun ascends, a gentle glow,
Painting the world in hues of snow.
Icicles drip, a symphony sings,
Of winter's touch and the joy it brings.

Footprints trace where few have tread,
In the soft powder, a path is spread.
The whispers of winds, a guiding hand,
Inviting all to explore this land.

Through frozen lakes, reflections gleam,
An enchanting, ephemeral dream.
Embrace the cold, feel the grace,
As winter's magic finds its place.

Crystal Reflections of a Winter's Gaze

Glimmers dance on the surface bright,
Mirrored wonders in soft twilight.
Each breath released, a cloud of mist,
In this realm, the heart can't resist.

Amongst the pines, shadows shift,
In their embrace, the spirits lift.
Snow blankets all in perfect peace,
Where worries fade, and sorrows cease.

The sun dips low, a tender sigh,
As twilight paints the evening sky.
Ice-kissed branches, a silver crown,
Nature's herald, a soft renown.

Frosty patterns, a fleeting art,
In quiet moments, the world takes heart.
As winter closes its gentle eyes,
The crystal reflections lift us high.

Beneath the Shimmering Frost

Beneath the frost, secrets lie,
Whispers of nature, a gentle sigh.
In every flake, a story spun,
Of winter nights and warmth begun.

The world asleep in a blanket white,
Glistening softly under twilight.
Stars twinkle down, a watchful gaze,
An eternal glow through the winter haze.

The chill may bite, but hearts are warm,
In the embrace of winter's charm.
As shadows lengthen, peace descends,
Bringing stillness that gently mends.

With every breath, the magic grows,
In every heart, true wonder flows.
Beneath the shimmering, gentle light,
We find our solace, pure delight.

Glimmers of Hope on White Pathways

In the stillness beneath the snow,
Glimmers of hope begin to show.
Footsteps crunch on paths of white,
Whispers of dreams take to flight.

The sun peeks through clouds so gray,
Guiding hearts on their way.
Each snowflake holds a tale,
Of love that shall never pale.

With every breath, a warmth ignites,
As spirits rise on frosty nights.
Together we walk hand in hand,
On sparkling trails, we bravely stand.

Nature's quilt, so pure and bright,
Wraps us in its soft delight.
With laughter echoing, joy's embrace,
We find ourselves in this sacred space.

In the distance, shadows play,
Where hope and beauty find their sway.
Trust the journey, take the leap,
Glimmers of hope, forever keep.

In Harmony with the Winter's Embrace

Under skies of shimmering gray,
Winter whispers, come and play.
Frosty branches, diamonds rare,
Nature's magic fills the air.

In quiet woods, the stillness breathes,
Where every twig and leaf believes.
Snowflakes dance on gentle breeze,
Creating harmony with such ease.

The world slows down, a perfect pause,
In this wonder, we find the cause.
To cherish moments, small and bright,
In winter's arms, we find our light.

Together, we gather near the fire,
Sharing dreams that never tire.
In this warmth, we feel alive,
In harmony, our spirits thrive.

As night falls, stars twinkle bright,
Guiding us with their soft light.
In winter's embrace, we stand free,
Together in this unity.

Breathing Dreams in a Frosty Haven

In a haven wrapped in frost's embrace,
We breathe in dreams at our own pace.
Whispered wishes float through the air,
In this quiet, there's magic to share.

The world seems hushed, wrapped in white,
Each breath becomes a soft delight.
Snowy pillows beneath our feet,
A sanctuary where hearts meet.

With every laugh, the silence sings,
Bringing joy on winter's wings.
In this frosty breath of night,
We find our hopes take glorious flight.

The moonlight dances on the snow,
Reflecting dreams we long to know.
In the quiet, our minds create,
Visions of love that simply await.

Together we find solace here,
Breathing dreams, casting fear.
In this haven, we hold the key,
To a winter's heart, wild and free.

Wonders Wrapped in a Winter's Embrace

A blanket of white, so pure, so bright,
Hides the wonders of winter's night.
Frosty breath hangs in the air,
Each moment filled with magic's stare.

Pine trees wear their snowy crown,
As we wander through the quiet town.
Chasing shadows, playing in light,
Wonders abound in the soft twilight.

Children laugh, their joy resounds,
As snowflakes swirl and tumble around.
In this frosty world of play,
Imagination finds its way.

With cups of cocoa, we gather tight,
Sharing stories through the night.
In warmth and laughter, we embrace,
The simple joys that time can't erase.

Wrapped in winter's soft caress,
We find ourselves in happiness.
Together, we celebrate the season's grace,
In the wonders wrapped in winter's embrace.

The Icy Hymn of Nightfall

Beneath the shroud of silvery grey,
Stars whisper softly, night leads the way.
Crystals glisten on the ground,
As shadows dance without a sound.

Cold winds weave through ancient trees,
Rustling leaves like whispered pleas.
Moonlight casts its ghostly glow,
Painting the world in frosty show.

Footsteps crunch on frozen trails,
Echoing through the winter gales.
Silent whispers fill the air,
Nature's hymn, a patient prayer.

In the stillness, time stands still,
As night invokes its icy thrill.
A heart beats slow, synced to the chill,
Amidst the shadows, dreams fulfill.

With every breath, the past awakes,
Memory mingles, silence breaks.
Embraced by night, the world forgets,
In this hymn, the soul begets.

Glacial Melodies of Yesterday's Chill

Echoes of laughter in the frost,
Memories linger, never lost.
Chilled whispers through the trees,
Calling softly, carried by the breeze.

Veils of silver hang in the air,
Forgotten moments, sweet and rare.
As daylight fades, the past appears,
Wrapped in stillness, calmed by fears.

Icicles play a silent tune,
Sparkling bright beneath the moon.
Each note dances on the wind,
Caressing shadows, love rescinds.

Winter's breath embraces tight,
Singing songs of pure delight.
Beneath the stars, we reminisce,
Finding solace in the abyss.

As time drifts on like falling snow,
We gather warmth from what we know.
In frozen hearts, the music glows,
Like hidden paths that winter shows.

Transcending into Glacial Whispers

In the silence of the night,
Breezes speak without a flight.
Glimmers of frost upon the ground,
Where secrets in shadows are found.

Frosted air, a gentle caress,
Wraps the earth in a stillness blessed.
Dreams emerge from frozen streams,
Flowing softly into our dreams.

Underneath the blanket of snow,
Past and present start to flow.
Visions dance in crystalline glow,
Telling tales we used to know.

In this world of softest white,
Whispers echo, pure and bright.
Each breath a mist, each hope a spark,
Illuminating the endless dark.

Transcending time, we chase the night,
In frosted realms, we find our light.
Glacial whispers soothe the soul,
In winter's embrace, we feel whole.

A Sigh of Winter in the Dusk

As dusk descends on barren lands,
Winter sighs, dusting the sands.
Crimson skies bow to the night,
In the silence, shadows take flight.

A chill creeps in with tender grace,
Embracing the world in gentle lace.
Frost-kissed breath escapes the lips,
Each moment holds the cold it grips.

Stars awaken in the twilight,
Glistening gems that cradle the night.
Hushed whispers merge in the air,
Singing softly, a melody rare.

Under the gaze of the glimmering stars,
Winter's sigh erases the scars.
Nature's rhythm beats with peace,
In the dusk, all worries cease.

Embracing stillness, hearts align,
In the chill, the soul starts to shine.
A sigh of winter, deep and profound,
In this quiet, true love is found.

The Enchantment of Icy Stillness

In the hush of winter's night,
Stars twinkle with pure delight.
Moonlight dances on the snow,
Whispers of the cold winds blow.

Trees wear cloaks of frosty lace,
Nature holds a tranquil space.
Silent echoes fill the air,
A beauty rare, beyond compare.

Footprints lead through icy trails,
Where the warmth of silence prevails.
Every breath a cloud of white,
In this magic, hearts take flight.

Glistening crystals catch the eye,
As the world breathes a gentle sigh.
Beauty wraps the earth so tight,
In the enchantment of the night.

Each moment feels like a dream,
In this serene, frozen scheme.
Colors muted, edges blurred,
In stillness, every soul is stirred.

Solitude in Frozen Landscapes

Amidst the white and endless scene,
Solitude in beauty's sheen.
A world untouched, all is bare,
In frosted silence, one can stare.

Snowflakes dance on winter's breath,
Marking the landscape's quiet death.
Each flake tells a story rare,
Of journeys taken, dreams laid bare.

Horizon stretches, vast and bold,
Whispers of the past unfold.
Footprints vanish, then appear,
In solitude, the heart feels clear.

Mountains wear their icy crowns,
Guardians of these frozen towns.
In the stillness, spirits roam,
Finding peace while far from home.

Embrace the quiet, let it in,
In frozen realms, the soul can grin.
Nature's beauty, stark yet grand,
In solitude, we fiercely stand.

Harmony in White-Chased Beauty

In blankets soft of purest white,
Harmony greets the fading light.
Each flake a note in nature's song,
Where we find that we belong.

Brushstrokes of the cold wind blow,
Painting all the land below.
Harmony rests beneath the frost,
In this stillness, none are lost.

A shimmering glow beneath the stars,
Echoes softly from afar.
The world adorned in sparkling grace,
In every corner, a sacred space.

Whispers of the winter's calm,
Wrapped in nature's quiet balm.
Here in stillness, hearts align,
In the lasting glow that shines.

Let the beauty of the white
Guide us softly through the night.
In this harmony we hold dear,
We find a love that conquers fear.

A Journey Through Frost's Embrace

A journey starts where shadows blend,
Into the frost where pathways end.
Steps are hushed on glistening ground,
In this magic, peace is found.

Each breath a ghost of winter's chill,
With every step, the heart can thrill.
Surrounded by the gentle glow,
In the realm of frost and snow.

Mountains rise like giants tall,
In their silence, we hear the call.
Through branches bare and skies so grey,
Nature beckons us to stay.

Fields sparkle in the morning light,
Frost's embrace feels warm and bright.
Every glance reveals a scene,
A story told, a dream routine.

As we move through this icy land,
With wonder, we take a stand.
In frost's embrace, we find our way,
A journey awaited, come what may.

Tracing Paths in White Wonders

Footprints carved in snow,
Whispers of the breeze,
Guiding souls that roam,
In a world of frozen trees.

Shadows dance on white,
Where the sun fades away,
Magic in the twilight,
Painting night from day.

Dreams unfold like maps,
Leaving trails to find,
Each turn a story,
In the heart and mind.

Laughter echoes bright,
Through the chilly air,
Binding friends together,
With a bond so rare.

Nature's gentle breath,
Calls the brave to play,
In a symphony of frost,
On this wintry day.

The Silent Symphony of Winter

Snowflakes fall like notes,
In a quiet, soft ballet,
Nature's whispered song,
As the world melts away.

Branches draped in white,
Strings of a frozen lyre,
Each flake tells a tale,
In the cold, they conspire.

Footprints mark the path,
A rhythm steady, true,
Echoes in the still,
As the winter winds blew.

Stars above like chimes,
In a night so deep,
Cradled in the hush,
Where the dreamers sleep.

Silence sings its notes,
In the glow of the moon,
Winter's symphony plays,
A timeless, quiet tune.

Celestial Dreams on a Frozen Canvas

Stars adorn the night,
Like diamonds on display,
Painting dreams in frost,
On this cold, bright day.

The moon, a silver brush,
Sweeps across the sky,
Creating realms of light,
Where imagined dreams lie.

Each flake a masterpiece,
With elegance and grace,
Nature's art unveiled,
In this tranquil space.

Whispers of the dawn,
Kiss the snowy ground,
Waking life anew,
In a world profound.

Celestial wonders twirl,
As the night takes flight,
Crafting visions pure,
In the heart of night.

Twilight's Kiss with the Crystal Moon

Twilight cloaks the land,
With a soft, gentle glow,
While shadows stretch long,
As the cool winds blow.

The crystal moon rises,
A guardian of dreams,
Bathing earth in silver,
As the starlight gleams.

Whispers fade to hush,
In this calming hour,
Nature holds its breath,
In winter's gentle power.

Reflections in the snow,
Dance of light and dark,
Each moment a treasure,
In the evening's spark.

Twilight's kiss lingers,
In the quiet night,
Underneath the heavens,
Everything feels right.

An Odyssey in the Glacial Mist

Through valleys deep, the shadows creep,
In icy breath, where secrets sleep.
Footsteps soft on powder's grace,
A whispered tale in frozen space.

The sky above, a canvas white,
Stars emerge in the frosty night.
Each breath a cloud, each glance a spark,
In night's embrace, we brave the dark.

Winds of change, so wild and free,
Guide us on this journey's spree.
Elusive paths, so faintly drawn,
We chase the light of the new dawn.

Reflections dance on rivers thin,
In glacial warmth, we feel the spin.
Visions swirl in sapphire gleam,
Reality blurs, caught in a dream.

So here we stand, with hearts ablaze,
Through frozen mists, in a blinding haze.
An odyssey, both fierce and bright,
In glacial mist, we find our light.

Frosty Pines and Distant Peaks

Amidst the pines, where silence reigned,
The frostbit air, our souls maintained.
Distant peaks, they touch the sky,
In winter's grip, we wander by.

Branches heavy with crystal weight,
Nature's art, we contemplate.
The whispering winds, they softly call,
In frosty splendor, we feel small.

Snowflakes dance on cheeks so cold,
Their gentle touch, a tale retold.
Each step we take, a fleeting trace,
In this realm, we find our place.

With every breath, a story spun,
Through frosty woods, our hearts are one.
The echo of the mountains' song,
In harmony, we all belong.

As twilight falls, the world aglow,
With frosty dreams, we choose to flow.
Amongst the pines, we seek the peaks,
In nature's whispers, our spirit speaks.

Beneath the Glare of Winter Bliss

Beneath the glare, where silence hums,
In winter's lap, our spirit drums.
The world ablaze in purest white,
In glacial grip, we find delight.

Icicles hang like crystal tears,
Glances shared through fleeting years.
In this embrace of frost and chill,
Our hearts ignite, our dreams fulfill.

The moonlight dances on snow-kissed ground,
In winter's bliss, true peace is found.
Each swirl of snow, a gentle sigh,
In the night sky, our wishes fly.

Branches laden with snowy lace,
In this enchanted, hallowed space.
Nature's beauty, we stand in awe,
In winter's realm, we grasp the law.

So let us wander through this night,
Beneath the glare, our souls take flight.
In winter bliss, we stake our claim,
In frost's embrace, we'll never be the same.

The Allure of Liquid Crystal

In the heart of the wild, a river gleams,
Flowing like liquid, a tapestry of dreams.
With every glance, the surface shimmers,
An allure that captivates and glimmers.

Surrounded by mountains, stark and bold,
A narrative woven, silently told.
The splash of water, a soft refrain,
In nature's song, we drift like rain.

Reflections dance on the watery skin,
Mirrors of life, where beauty begins.
Rivers unravel the stories of old,
Where secrets of earth, in silence unfold.

Glistening drops catch the light of day,
A melody flows, leading the way.
In every ripple, a tale unfolds,
Of journeys carved in whispers bold.

So let us savor this liquid grace,
In nature's arms, we find our place.
The allure of crystal, forever in reach,
In every heartbeat, a lesson to teach.

Moonlit Rapture in Stillness

In silver glow the shadows dance,
A whispered waltz in night's expanse.
Each star a beacon, softly bright,
Guiding dreams through endless night.

Beneath the trees, the silence hums,
Nature's song, a heart that strums.
With every breeze, the world unwinds,
A tapestry of gentle finds.

Moonbeams touch the cool, wet ground,
In this embrace, all peace is found.
Time stands still, the moment grand,
An echo soft, a lover's hand.

A symphony of night unfolds,
As stories lost in starlight told.
Each breath a promise, soft and clear,
In moonlit rapture, hearts draw near.

With every sigh, the world must pause,
In stillness deep, we find our cause.
A realm where dreams and silence meet,
In whispered vows, we find our beat.

Carried on the Breath of Winter

As snowflakes fall, a silent crowd,
The earth is wrapped in nature's shroud.
Each flake a whisper, pure and bright,
A fleeting glimpse of pure delight.

The air is crisp, like whispered dreams,
Flowing softly with silver streams.
Breath turns to mist in frosty air,
A dance of warmth in winter's stare.

Footsteps crunch on the powdered street,
A symphony beneath each beat.
The world transformed, a canvas white,
In winter's grip, all feels just right.

Beneath the moon, the shadows play,
Carried by winds that never sway.
They weave through trees, a ghostly thread,
In quiet nights where dreams are fed.

Wrapped in coats of wool and care,
We wander forth, the frosty air.
With every breath, we claim the night,
In winter's arms, the heart takes flight.

Elysian Fields of White

Where daisies bloom in fields of gold,
The sun spills warmth, a sight to hold.
Each petal dances in the breeze,
A symphony beneath the trees.

In this fair land, the moments gleam,
As hearts entwine in a golden dream.
A soft embrace, a time so right,
In Elysian fields, all takes flight.

The sky paints hues of softest blue,
As love unfolds, so pure and true.
With laughter ringing through the air,
A canvas bright, beyond compare.

As twilight falls, the stars appear,
Each twinkle holds a whispered cheer.
In fields of white, our hopes ignite,
A tapestry of hearts in flight.

In laughter's echo, love will seize,
In every moment, the heart's unease.
Here, in this place, our spirits sing,
In Elysian fields, life takes wing.

Shivers Beneath a Twilight Sky

As dusk descends with velvet grace,
The world transforms, a soft embrace.
Colors bleed into twilight's hue,
A canvas wide with dreams anew.

Each whisper of the cooling air,
A secret shared, beyond compare.
In shades of violet, night takes hold,
The stars emerge, a tale untold.

Beneath the sky where shadows play,
We chase the dreams that drift away.
In twilight's breath, we pause and sigh,
With shivers felt, we wonder why.

The moon begins its watchful rise,
A guardian of our whispered lies.
With every heartbeat, time stands still,
In twilight's arms, we feel the thrill.

As night enfolds the weary day,
We find our peace in shadows' sway.
With every glance, the heart draws nigh,
In twilight's breath, we dare to fly.

Waving Goodbyes to the Warm

The sun descends, a gentle sigh,
Bright days fade, as shadows lie.
Leaves are crisp, the air turns bold,
We gather memories, stories told.

Embers dance in a fading glow,
Whispers of warmth as breezes flow.
Hands held tight, we share a glance,
In the chill, we find our chance.

Stars awaken, the night unfolds,
Familiar tales, in hearts retold.
Every moment, a fleeting game,
A soft farewell, the warmth, the same.

With heavy hearts, we drift away,
Wrapped in dreams of yesterday.
But as we part, with love, we bind,
The essence of warmth still in our mind.

So we wave goodbyes, our spirits near,
In winter's embrace, we'll persevere.
For every chill that casts a shadow,
Beats a heart that knows tomorrow.

Frosted Horizons Beyond the Pines

Beyond the pines, a world transformed,
A canvas white, where dreams are formed.
Frosted whispers on branches sway,
Nature's breath in winter's play.

Crystal flakes drift through the air,
A wonderland that few may share.
Each step a crunch, a sound so bright,
Underneath the moon's soft light.

Horizon glows, a silver sheen,
Where shadows dance, and hearts convene.
Every glimmer speaks of hope,
In this chill, our spirits cope.

The world laid bare, so pure, so vast,
A reminder of the seasons past.
Together we roam, hand in hand,
A frosted dreamscape, nature planned.

In silence, we find beauty rare,
With every breath, a soothing air.
Frosted horizons, our souls unite,
In winter's arms, we feel the light.

A Serenade of Ice and Light

Underneath a sapphire sky,
Icicles dangle, snowflakes fly.
A serenade of crackling sound,
In this frozen realm, joy is found.

Light dances softly on icy streams,
Weaving through the land of dreams.
Whispers of winter, sweet and low,
A melody only true hearts know.

With every step, the world sings clear,
In frost-kissed air, there's nothing to fear.
Nature's concert, magic spun,
A lullaby till day is done.

The stars twinkle with a knowing gaze,
Embracing the night in a silvery haze.
Together we drift beneath the skies,
Captured in the moment, where time flies.

So let this serenade take flight,
In the heart of winter's night.
As long as we share this winter sight,
We'll forever dance, in ice and light.

Moonlight on a Shimmering Landscape

Moonlight spills on the sleeping earth,
Banishing shadows, revealing worth.
The landscape shimmers, dressed in white,
A tranquil scene, a perfect night.

Silver beams caress the trees,
A soft embrace in the winter breeze.
Every branch a glint, a spark,
Nature whispers in the dark.

Footsteps echo on frosty ground,
In this silence, peace is found.
Underneath the starry dome,
Every heart feels a sense of home.

With every breath, the world aglow,
Casting dreams in the moonlit show.
We are but travelers in night's grace,
Caught in the beauty of time and space.

So let us gather these moments dear,
In the glow of the moon's soft sphere.
For as long as light can softly play,
We'll cherish nights that lead our way.

www.ingramcontent.com/pod-product-compliance
Ingram Content Group UK Ltd.
Pitfield, Milton Keynes, MK11 3LW, UK
UKHW031940151224
452382UK00006B/231